ALABASTER

Published in Los Angeles by Alabaster Creative Inc.

Printed in China
through Asia Pacific Offset

Contact
hello@alabasterco.com
www.alabasterco.com

Founded in 2016. Based in Los Angeles.

The 7
LAST SAYINGS
of JESUS

INTRODUCTION

*"So the Word became human
and made his home among us.
He was full of unfailing love and
faithfulness. And we have seen
his glory, the glory of
the Father's one and only Son."*

JOHN 1:14, NLT

There is an obvious weight and import placed upon the words of Jesus. So-called "red letter Bibles" visually emphasize Jesus' sayings, ensuring they stand out from the surrounding text and reminding readers of their significance. The opening chapter of John's gospel goes so far as to describe Jesus himself as the Word of God embodied—divine mission and intention incarnate. The takeaway is clear: when Jesus speaks, we do well to listen.

Jesus said many things that we hold dear—famous teachings, such as the Sermon on the Mount, and illuminating parables, such as the story of the Good Samaritan. But some of the most well-known and oft-quoted expressions come at the culmination of his earthly ministry: his crucifixion. The practice of reflecting on the Last Sayings of Christ—the seven expressions biblically attributed to Jesus on the cross—has long been associated with the lead-up to Easter, offering a mindful approach to navigating the Lenten period. But whatever the season, they offer wisdom and insight. Each of these quotations, carefully recorded by the gospel writers, reveals something about Jesus' character. They illuminate the importance and purpose of the cross. When we take the time to ruminate on these words carefully, we gain insight into the nature of our Savior and deepen our relationship with him.

To that end, we offer *The 7 Last Sayings of Jesus,* a 40-day devotional centered around the final words spoken by Jesus during his time on earth. Perfect for Lenten study, but ready to use all year round. Featuring eight reflections each rooted in a different biblical phrase (the traditional seven spoken from the cross and a final reflection on the words spoken at the Ascension), this book is intended to draw us closer to Christ. We jump into Jesus' story *in media res*, after the Last Supper, Gethsemane, and his arrest. These are words spoken by a Christ who is enduring an arduous ordeal. And yet, there is wisdom and hope to discover. Alongside these reflections, we've included 40 thoughtful prompts that encourage daily contemplation, as well as prayers offered out of the lessons gleaned from each of Jesus' sayings.

May this devotional enrich our faith and open our hearts and minds more fully to the miraculous and generous work of Jesus. *Amen.*

TABLE *of* CONTENTS

01

JESUS *FORGIVES*

The SEVEN
LAST SAYINGS
of JESUS

Father, forgive them, for they do not know what they are doing.

LUKE 23:34

Jesus *Forgives*

*"Jesus said, '**Father, forgive them, for they do not know what they are doing.**' And they divided up his clothes by casting lots."*

LUKE 23:34, NIV

We know all too well that forgiveness can be a challenging process. Even in the best of circumstances, when we have the time and space to heal, when those who have wronged us apologize and make amends, letting go of our pain isn't easy. To forgive can feel akin to eating our vegetables or exercising—something we know we ought to do for our good, but not something we relish.

This makes the forgiveness Jesus extends on the cross all the more astonishing. He forgives in the moment of wrongdoing, even as the crowd mocks and harms him. This is a radical expression of mercy. Instead of condemning those participating in his suffering, Jesus intercedes on their behalf. He doesn't wait for repentance, but offers grace freely.

While we tend to associate forgiveness with justice—as something that comes *after* wrongs have been righted—Jesus' mercy is proactive. It does not dismiss or ignore the harm done, but seeks healing even in the face of that harm. Christ's grace is not a passive forgiveness, a formal pardon granted by rote. It is active, intentional, and undeserved.

"Father, forgive them, for they do not know what they are doing." Through these words, we glimpse the full scope and scale of the redemptive work of the cross. In a single sentence, Jesus fulfills the heart of the Gospel—that God does not abandon us in our sin but moves toward us in love, drawing all things back into communion. This sacrifice conquers every transgression, not just in the past and future, but even in the present moment of torment. The cross assures us that no one is beyond forgiveness. If Jesus' mercy can extend to those jeering at his pain and seeking profit from his suffering, it can reach us too. This is the kind of forgiveness that meets us in our weakest moments—when we lash out, when we stumble, when we turn away. We are not required to clean ourselves up first. We are simply called to return.

Furthermore, the forgiveness Jesus extends is personal and relational. It is offered not from a place of superiority, but from one of care. Even in his pain, Christ recognizes that the cruelty and carelessness of humanity is to our own detriment as well as his. He knows that so much of human sin is rooted in negligence—misunderstanding, fear, woundedness. Jesus sees beyond the offense to the fractured places that drive it. He knows our limitations, our confusion, our desperate need for healing, and chooses mercy. This radical mercy is a selfless act of love from our Good Shepherd. Amid his agony, his heart breaks not for himself, but for his lost and misguided sheep.

Each of us can likely draw to mind moments when we've acted without knowing what we are doing—unwittingly hurting others, falling short, or turning away from God. Jesus does not condemn us for these mistakes, but graciously seeks to open our eyes and guide us forward with compassion. Out of this example, we can reframe our own approach to forgiveness. We can strive to adopt a Christ-like posture of mercy. We can release the grudges, grievances, or offenses we're clinging to. May we receive this mercy with open hands and extend it with open hearts. For in following the way of Jesus, we do not excuse wrongdoing, but choose to live as people of grace.

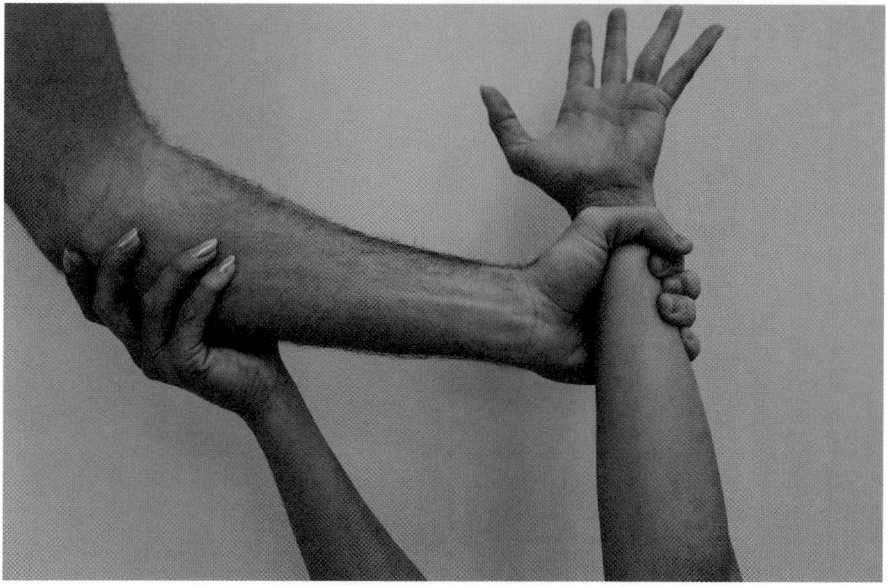

Daily Prompts

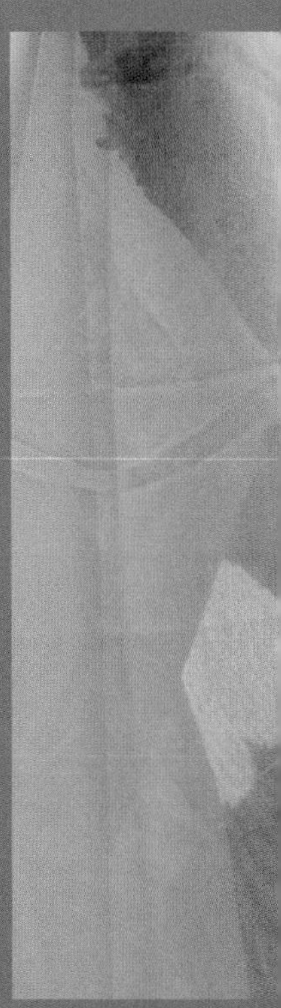

Day 1

What barriers—emotional, relational, or spiritual—make it difficult for you to offer forgiveness freely?

Day 2

When have you experienced forgiveness in a way that felt undeserved? What did that moment reveal to you about grace?

Day 3

How does Jesus' act of forgiving amid his suffering challenge your assumptions about when or how forgiveness should be given?

Day 4

How might your life change if you truly believed you are already fully seen, fully known, and still fully forgiven?

Day 5

Think of someone who has wounded you. Without rushing to resolution, how might you begin to pray for them?

Prayer

Jesus, your mercy meets us even in our thoughtlessness and failure. Teach us to receive your forgiveness with humility and to extend it with grace. Soften our hearts where they've grown hard, and help us walk in your way of radical compassion, love, and mercy.

Amen.

02

JESUS *RESTORES*

The SEVEN
LAST SAYINGS
of JESUS

Truly I tell you,
today you will be with me in paradise.

LUKE 23:43

Jesus *Restores*

"But the other criminal rebuked him. 'Don't you fear God,' he said, 'since you are under the same sentence? We are punished justly, for we are getting what our deeds deserve. But this man has done nothing wrong.' Then he said, 'Jesus, remember me when you come into your kingdom.' Jesus answered him, ***'Truly I tell you, today you will be with me in paradise.'"***

LUKE 23:40-43, NIV

Even hanging on the cross, his body is wracked with pain, Jesus remains who he has always been: the One who sees, saves, and restores. His focus is not on proving his innocence or lashing out at those who mock him. Instead, in his final hours, he turns toward another man—broken, condemned, and only moments from death.

Two criminals hang beside Jesus, both guilty, both hopeless. One joins in the crowd's scorn, while the other speaks words of humility and trust: *"Jesus, remember me when you come into your kingdom."* It is not a polished prayer, accompanied by years of faithfulness, religious devotion, or moral reform. It is a desperate plea—fragile and imperfect, but honest. This man is all too aware of his shortcomings—he even declares the cross a just punishment for his actions. Nevertheless, he asks for Jesus' remembrance, that whatever righteous work Jesus is doing might include him as well. With authority and compassion, Jesus responds:

"*Truly* I tell you,
today you will be *with me*
in paradise."

It's more than
mere comfort;
this is a *sweeping promise*
of restoration, belonging,
and eternal life.

In *this moment,*
the condemned man
does not receive what
he "deserves"
but what only
grace can give.

Jesus does not demand proof of repentance, a spotless past, or a future of good works. He does not measure worthiness by human standards. If the gift of the cross had to be earned, none of us would receive it. Jesus simply hears the man's cry and answers with tenderness and inclusion. Our Redeemer acts decisively, bridging the gap between guilt and glory. This is who Jesus continues to be for us. His restoration is not bound by time, failure, or circumstance. It is not too late. It is not too messy. We are not beyond his reach. Whether we come to him in the strength of lifelong faith or in the trembling hope of a spur-of-the-moment prayer, his response is the same: restoration. We are seen; we are remembered; we are being made new.

Jesus does not restore from a distance; he draws near. He offers not only a future hope but a present belonging. We are not left to wonder if his grace will be enough—it already is. We are not left to wander alone—he himself is with us.

Christ sees us clearly, in both our brokenness and our desire for him. He responds with mercy, not condemnation. He welcomes the lost, strengthens the weary, and carries us into the fullness of life that God intends. When we turn to Jesus, even falteringly, we are met by the same Savior who welcomed a dying man to paradise. His promise then is his promise now: in him, our story does not end in despair, but in restoration.

Daily Prompts

Day 1

Have you ever felt forgotten by Jesus? How might this passage offer reassurance?

Day 2

How does this passage challenge the way you think about God's grace, especially in light of your own shortcomings?

Day 3

What areas of your life feel beyond restoration right now? How might Jesus be inviting you to trust him with those places?

Day 4

In what ways might God be calling you to let go of striving and simply rest in mercy?

Day 5

Jesus promised, *"Today you will be with me in paradise."* How does Jesus' immediate assurance of intimacy reshape how you understand his presence in your daily life?

Prayer

Lord Jesus, you see us in our brokenness and still speak words of hope. Thank you for restoring what feels beyond repair, for welcoming us into your presence, and for offering paradise even in our darkest hour. Teach us to trust your mercy and walk in your restoring love.

Amen.

03

JESUS *PROVIDES*

The SEVEN
LAST SAYINGS
of JESUS

Dear woman, here is your son...
Here is your mother.

JOHN 19:25–27

Jesus *Provides*

"Standing near the cross were Jesus' mother, and his mother's sister, Mary (the wife of Clopas), and Mary Magdalene. When Jesus saw his mother standing there beside the disciple he loved, he said to her, ***'Dear woman, here is your son.'*** *And he said to this disciple,* ***'Here is your mother.'*** *And from then on this disciple took her into his home."*

JOHN 19:25-27, NLT

Reflecting on the gift Jesus extends to us on the cross, it's easy for this miracle to feel ephemeral. We speak of the forgiveness of sins—of restoration into eternity. These truths are vast and vital, worthy of every meditation and praise. And yet, at times, they can feel distant—grand in scope but somehow removed from the ordinary patterns of our lives. We may get the impression that Jesus is only concerned with our heavenly souls, with redemption on a cosmic scale. The words of John 19:25-27 shatter this assumption.

Amid excruciating pain, Jesus does not merely look to the sweeping work of salvation; he turns his attention to his mother. He sees her standing there in her grief, vulnerable and uncertain about what comes next. In his final breaths, Jesus forges a new family, entrusting Mary to the beloved disciple, John, and John to Mary. *"Here is your son... here is your mother."* Words simple in form, yet weighty in meaning. Words that tether heavenly redemption to earthly care. This is not a small detail tucked into the crucifixion narrative. It is a poignant glimpse into the heart of

Jesus. In this moment, Jesus reminds us that his provision isn't just ethereal or spiritual. His love is not merely future-oriented; it is embodied, relational, and deeply present. Even as he carries the burden of the world's sin, he notices the practical needs of his mother for safety, companionship, and belonging. He sees the needs of those he holds dear and responds with foresight, compassion, and love.

This blessing neither began nor ended on the cross. Provision and care for others were hallmarks of his earthly ministry—from healing the sick to feeding crowds to welcoming the outcasts. This is a continuation of that same posture. Jesus sees Mary's need. He sees John's need. And he meets them both with care.

"*Here* is your son...
here is your mother."

In *this moment,* Jesus reminds us
that his provision isn't just
ethereal or spiritual.
His love is not merely
future-oriented; *it is*
embodied, relational,
and deeply *present.*

In the same way, Jesus sees us. He knows the concerns that weigh heavily on our hearts—the relationships we carry, the fears we harbor, the quiet places where we yearn for belonging. Just as he attended to Mary in her sorrow, he attends to us in ours. His love is not only for eternity but also for the provision of the practical needs of today: comfort, connection, care, and community.

Jesus' love shows up in the details of our lives, in the needs we scarcely voice, in the bonds of care he continues to form. At the cross we see, perhaps more clearly than anywhere else, that God's provision is both cosmic and personal—vast enough to hold the universe, yet tender enough to notice a grieving mother and ensure she is not left alone.

To follow Jesus is to join him in this work of creating family where there is none, offering care where there is need, and embodying love in both small and significant ways. The redemption offered by Christ is not only about heaven someday—it is about how we live and love today.

Daily Prompts

Day 1

What strikes you most about Jesus caring for his mother even while carrying the weight of the cross?

Day 2

How does this moment challenge the way you think about what it means for God to "provide"?

Day 3

When have you felt unseen in your needs, and how might this passage reassure you that Jesus notices and cares?

Day 4

What does Jesus' creation of a new family teach us about belonging to the body of Christ?

Day 5

In what ways can you join Jesus in embodying his love—meeting the practical, everyday needs of those around you with compassion and intentionality?

Prayer

Jesus, even from the cross, you noticed and provided. You saw the needs of Mary and John, and you extended love and care to them. Help us trust that you are reaching out to us, too—in our fears, our longings, our daily lives. Teach us to embody your tender provision for others.

Amen.

04

JESUS *LAMENTS*

My God, my God,
why have you forsaken me?

MARK 15:34

Jesus *Laments*

"At noon, darkness came over the whole land until three in the afternoon. And at three in the afternoon Jesus cried out in a loud voice, 'Eloi, Eloi, lema sabachthani?' (which means ***'My God, my God, why have you forsaken me?'****)."*

MARK 15:33-34, NIV

Faith is a source of strength and blessing to us as we navigate this life. But, as believers, we may sometimes feel ashamed of our darker emotions. We rush through sadness, suppress anger, and grasp for the bright side, as though naming our despair, confusion, or rage signals a lack of trust in God. Yet scripture tells another story. There is room for lament—space to bring our raw, unfiltered cries before the Lord. On the cross, Jesus himself models this, showing us that giving voice to honest sorrow can itself be an act of faith.

As the ordeal of crucifixion drags on, Jesus doesn't hide his anguish. He cries out to God, not in quiet, serene prayer, but giving full voice to his misery and spiritual desolation: *"My God, my God, why have you forsaken me?"* Jesus draws upon the longstanding history of lament as a cornerstone of our relationship with our Creator. This plea originates in Psalm 22, penned by King David, and in quoting it, Jesus harkens back to generations of people who brought their grief before God.

Pain and sorrow
are not barriers to the Father,

but realities that Christ
lays at the Lord's feet.

For lament is a long tradition; we are never the first to cry out—our voices join a chorus stretching back through time. It is a sacred expression of grief and confusion directed toward God. For Jesus, the world is quite literally dark, the pain immeasurable. Yet even in this suffering, even feeling abandoned, he reaches toward God. Pain and sorrow are not barriers to the Father, but realities that Christ lays at the Lord's feet.

With this impassioned cry, Jesus demonstrates that lament is not weakness—it is a faithful, courageous act. It holds paradox—distance and intimacy, doubt and faith, despair and trust—in the same breath. We can remain tethered to God even when we feel far away. We do not need to hide our doubts or sanitize our prayers. God can hold our rawest emotions. To ask God into our grief as Jesus does connects us to God even in moments when things feel silent, dark, or unfair. We can also look to the fullness of Psalm 22 for encouragement. Though it begins with despair, this psalm of David moves toward hope and praise.[1] Jesus' invocation here on the cross hints at this trajectory: lament is not the end of the story but part of the journey of being made whole by God.

In Jesus, we have a Savior who not only hears our cries but has cried out himself. He invites us to face our pain—not alone, but alongside him. Lament does not mean a loss of faith; it is often the soil in which abiding trust is planted. Our honest reckoning allows space to process our feelings; it drives us to pause and abide in God rather than barreling ahead in search of resolution. When we bring our hurts to Jesus, we are not met with shame, but with deep and compassionate understanding.

[1] Psalm 22:24, NLT.

Daily Prompts

Day 1

When have you felt that God was silent or distant? What did you do with those feelings, and what might it look like to bring them honestly to God now?

Day 2

Darkness covered the land as Jesus cried out.[2] How might external circumstances in your life mirror the darkness that Jesus experienced?

---

[2] Mark 15:33

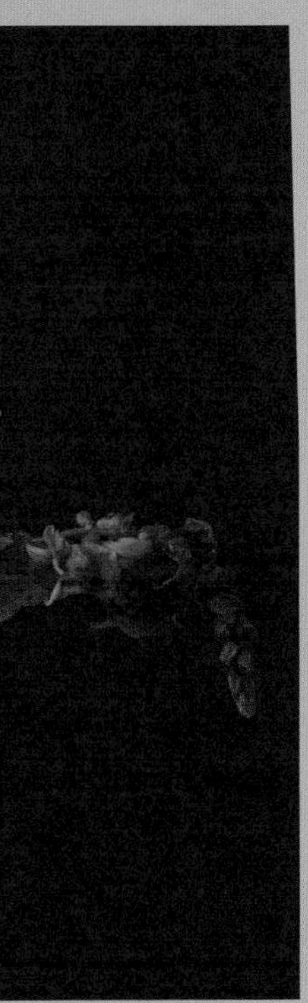

Day 3

How does considering the long history of lament affect the way you view your own struggles?

Day 4

What practices or prayers could help you keep turning toward God when despair tempts you to turn away?

Day 5

How does knowing that Jesus, too, has voiced feelings of abandonment change the way you experience and express your own grief?

Prayer

Christ, you entered the shadows and gave voice to grief. Teach us to trust that our laments are safe in your hands. When we feel abandoned, remind us that even in silence, you are near, weaving sorrow into the soil of deeper faith.

Amen.

05

JESUS *UNDERSTANDS*

The SEVEN
LAST SAYINGS
of JESUS
I am thirsty.
JOHN 19:28–29

Jesus *Understands*

*"Jesus knew that his mission was now finished, and to fulfill Scripture he said, **'I am thirsty.'** A jar of sour wine was sitting there, so they soaked a sponge in it, put it on a hyssop branch, and held it up to his lips."*

JOHN 19:28-29, NLT

The world can be a big and frightening place, filled with global crises and non-stop breaking news. There is no shortage of larger-than-life problems or existential questions. But sometimes—oftentimes even—we can't bring ourselves to engage with such things. Our day-to-day concerns are more than enough to worry about. Getting enough sleep, ensuring our families are fed, and making it through school and work weeks are already tall orders. We're focused on survival.

Despite what we may assume, Jesus understands these base-level concerns. The ordeal of the crucifixion is one of both spiritual struggle and physical exhaustion, leaving him aching and parched. Our God doesn't bypass human pain but enters into it completely. *"I am thirsty."* Such a simple phrase; one might wonder why the gospel writers bothered recording it. Yet these words serve two purposes.

First, they fulfill a scriptural prophecy—*"But instead, they give me poison for food; they offer me sour wine for my thirst."*[3] Even in this moment of fragility, Jesus is carrying forward the story of God's redemption. Additionally, these words reveal Jesus' deep identification with human need. He knows what it means to be worn down by the weight of life. Jesus didn't just suffer in theory—he felt it viscerally: the sting of betrayal, the weight of fatigue, the thirst of a weary body.

[3] Psalm 69:21, NLT.

This is striking vulnerability, particularly when juxtaposed with societal demands for strength and stoicism. Most of us try to hide our need—we mask our exhaustion, dismiss our limits, or push ourselves to keep going. To say "I am thirsty" is to admit frailty, to acknowledge dependence. Jesus' willingness to speak this truth reminds us that our needs do not disqualify us from God's presence. Instead, they can become a place of encounter. A faint plea for a drink becomes a bridge between his experience and ours. When we are exhausted, grieving, or overwhelmed, we do not cry out to a distant God—we cry out to One who knows. Jesus intimately understands the body's aches and the pangs of hunger. His empathy is not abstract—it is lived. And in him, we find rest and understanding that runs deeper than words. When we feel stretched thin or unseen, Jesus meets us with knowing eyes.

The *goodness* and *glory*

of God's kingdom

encompass a *defeat*
of crying and pain

as well as sin and death.

We cannot pretend that we are lone islands, disconnected from the concerns of the world. It is precisely these everyday survival concerns that connect us all together. Yes, the work of the cross and the wonder of the empty tomb have salvific and everlasting implications—God cares for the entirety of creation. But woven into this work is also a deep empathy for the earthly challenges of being human. The big picture and the small scale are inextricably linked; neither supercedes the other. The goodness and glory of God's Kingdom defeat crying and pain as well as sin and death.[4]

Jesus' thirst dignifies our own cries of need. He invites us to bring our burdens into his presence. And in doing so, he meets us with the assurance that he has known thirst, too, and that one day, every longing will be satisfied by the everlasting waters he provides.[5]

[4] Revelation 21:4, NLT.

[5] John 4:13–14, NLT.

Daily Prompts

Day 1

What simple needs in your own life do you hesitate to name before God, and why?

Day 2

How might Jesus' willingness to admit thirst free you to embrace your own vulnerability instead of hiding it?

Day 3

Where in your daily routines—sleep, meals, work, family—do you most feel the weight of being human, and how might you invite Christ's presence into those moments?

Day 4

What does it mean to you that Jesus chose to fulfill his mission not in strength but in weakness and need?

Day 5

How can Jesus' empathy shape the way you respond to others who are weary, hungry, or overlooked?

Prayer

Jesus, you know what it is to thirst, to hunger, to grow weary. Thank you for entering our humanity so fully that nothing we carry is foreign to you. Meet us in our weakness with empathy. Teach us to rest in your nearness and extend your care to others.

Amen.

06

JESUS *TRIUMPHS*

It is finished!

JOHN 19:30

Jesus *Triumphs*

"When Jesus had tasted it, he said,
'It is finished!'
Then he bowed his head and gave up his spirit."

JOHN 19:30, NLT

Reading the account of Jesus' final moments, it can be easy to misread this scene as one of defeat—a weary pronouncement of *"It is finished"* before finally succumbing to death. At first glance, it can seem as though the weight of the world has finally crushed him. The burden is too great. The forces of hate, sin, and death are too powerful. That's certainly how any of us would feel in such a circumstance. Our personal struggles and communal trials often seem insurmountable. Conquering death? Restoring a broken world? Those are grand, lofty ideals—but not likely realities.

And yet, "It is finished" is not a whisper of resignation. It is a pronouncement of resolution. Jesus does not say, "I am finished," as if he has been worn down and overcome. He says, *"It is finished"*—the work he came to do has been accomplished. The cross, once a symbol of shame and intimidation, becomes a symbol of victory. The very instrument of his humiliation transforms into a declaration that sin is defeated, death disarmed, and love triumphant.

As we've seen throughout the weeks of this devotional, this victory is both cosmic and intimate. Biblically, Jesus' death marks the completion of God's redemptive plan, the fulfillment of prophecy, and the inauguration of a new creation. And we, personally, have cause for celebration. We are the recipients of this finished work. The debt that we could never pay is wiped clean. Salvation is not something we must fight to earn—it is a gift already secured by Christ.

The cross,
once a symbol of shame
and intimidation,
becomes a symbol of *victory.*

The very instrument
of his humiliation
transforms into a *declaration*
that sin is defeated, death disarmed,
and love triumphant.

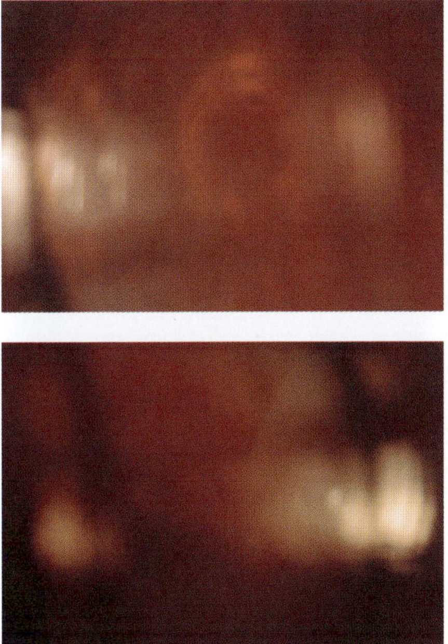

Jesus' words usher in freedom for all of humanity. We need no longer strive for redemption or wrestle endlessly with the fear that our efforts are insufficient. Instead, we are invited to live out of the assurance that Jesus restores us to the Kingdom. Grace is no longer a promise to hope for; it is a truth to enter into. Our daily lives, with all their anxieties, temptations, and trials, are held within the context of that victory. We are called to step into freedom and gratitude, to move forward with the confidence of one who has been redeemed.

Living in the light of Jesus' triumph transforms how we respond to setbacks, failures, and fears. When we stumble or grow weary, we remember that the ultimate work has been done. When the world seems unkind or chaotic, we can rest in the reality that love has already won.

Today, *"It is finished"* is not just a biblical quote; it is an invitation. What could life look like if we lived as ones already redeemed? Jesus' triumph on the cross is not only a past event to remember—it is a present reality to inhabit, moment by moment, choice by choice, in gratitude, hope, and love.

Daily Prompts

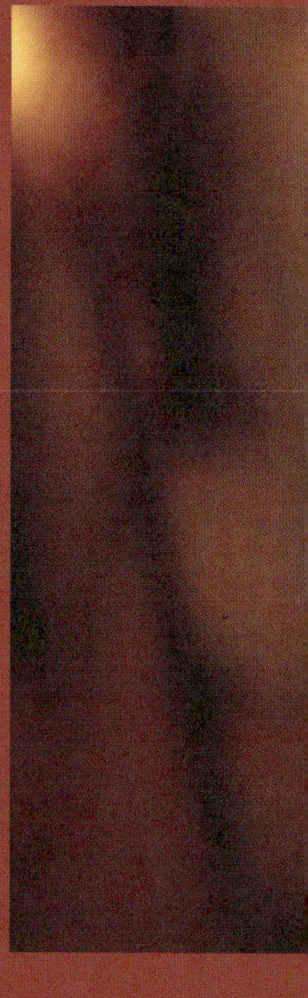

Day 1

Reflect on the moments that have felt like personal triumphs. Where was God in those moments?

Day 2

Jesus' triumph transforms the cross from a symbol of shame into a symbol of victory. How might this change the way you approach challenges or hardships in your own life?

Day 3

What would it look like to carry the reality of Christ's triumph into your thoughts, words, and decisions this week?

Day 4

Understanding the triumph of the cross means relying on Jesus' strength over our own. Where can you lean more fully on him?

Day 5

What does it look like for you to embody gratitude and freedom today, knowing the victory has already been won?

Prayer

Lord Jesus, your work is finished and the victory is secure. Help us to live not in striving or fear, but in the freedom and gratitude of redemption. Teach us to walk daily in the reality of your triumph, trusting your love in every moment.

Amen.

07

JESUS *WITH GOD*

Father, into your hands
I commit my spirit.

LUKE 23:46-47

Jesus *With God*

"Jesus called out with a loud voice,
'Father, into your hands I commit my spirit.'
When he had said this, he breathed his last. The centurion, seeing what had happened, praised God and said, 'Surely this was a righteous man.'"

LUKE 23:46-47, NIV

"Father, into your hands I commit my spirit." A simple phrase with resounding implications: even in death, Jesus is not alone. He is fully, completely, indivisibly with God. After hours of suffering, betrayal, and apparent abandonment, his final utterance is one of intimacy and communion, a return to the source of his life and strength—his Father.

From the beginning, Jesus' life was defined by this connection. He lived in constant fellowship with God, declaring, "*The Father and I are one.*"[6] Even at the threshold of death, that connection is not severed. His spirit, tenderly and trustingly placed into God's hands, demonstrates that the bond between Father and Son is eternal, unshaken by pain or fear. In his darkest moment, Jesus remains with God, and through him, we are invited into that same presence.

[6] John 10:30, NLT.

To *entrust* his spirit
to the Lord
is not to abandon hope
but to
fully embrace
the security of being held.

This is unmatched intimacy. To entrust his spirit to the Lord is not to abandon hope but to fully embrace the security of being held. Jesus dies not in despair, but in the confidence of belovedness. In his final breath, he models for us what it means to abide in God: to rest fully in the care, wisdom, and love of the Creator, knowing that nothing—death, sin, or suffering—can separate us from God's presence.

Even those on the outside can perceive the power and integrity in Jesus' trust. The centurion who witnessed this scene responds with awe: *"Surely this was a righteous man."* While we might expect a man in Jesus' situation to be struck silent, this final pronouncement is boldly and loudly declared. Understanding that he has been and always will be with God, Jesus exits his mortal life calmly and confidently.

Jesus' final words challenge us to reconsider what it means to be with God ourselves. To commit our spirits into God's hands is not to relinquish life but to cherish it fully—held in the constant, tender embrace of the Father. This posture transforms how we view fear, failure, and loss. To live in God's presence is to know that we are never abandoned, that even in our darkest moments, we are secure, loved, and known.

Today, Jesus invites us into the same reality: to walk not apart from God, but with Him, every moment, every breath. To be with God is to experience the peace, strength, and belonging that surpass all understanding. In life, in death, and in every uncertainty between, we are never outside the reach of our Father's presence.

Abiding in God's care does not mean we avoid pain or hardship. It means that in the midst of life's trials, we can rely on our relationship with God to keep us going, knowing that our spirits are treasured, our lives are known, and our hearts are beloved. To live this way is to live fully, faithfully, and without fear, wrapped in the embrace of divine love that never falters, from the first breath to the last.

Daily Prompts

Day 1

How do Jesus' final words shape your understanding of what it means to be fully with God?

Day 2

In what areas of your life do you struggle to feel God's presence? Invite God to meet you there.

Day 3

How does the assurance that Jesus is with God shape your faith experience?

Day 4

How might seeing Jesus' intimacy with the Father change the way you approach prayer, relationship, or your own moments of suffering?

Day 5

What does it mean for you personally to live each day knowing that being "with God" is possible in both life's triumphs and trials?

Prayer

Jesus, in your final breath, you showed us the sweetness of being with God. Help us to lay our lives open-handedly into the Father's care, to rest in your presence, and to walk each day knowing that in every sorrow, every joy, and every moment, we are held and beloved.

Amen.

08

JESUS *WITH US*

I am with you always, even to the end of the age.

MATTHEW 28:20

Jesus *With Us*

"Teach these new disciples to obey all the commands I have given you. And be sure of this: ***I am with you always, even to the end of the age."***

MATTHEW 28:20, NLT.

Reflecting on Jesus' last words to his disciples before ascending to Heaven—*"I am with you always, even to the end of the age"*—it's easy to feel wistful. We imagine the wonder of physically walking alongside him, hearing his voice, witnessing his miracles. Perhaps we long for Heaven, where we will dwell fully in his presence. We might envy the disciples who lived with him, marveling at the intimacy they experienced.

And yet, Jesus is not distant. His presence is not confined to memory, imagination, or future hope. He is with us—tangibly, actively, here and now.

These words are not a poetic flourish or an abstract theological statement. They are a living promise: Jesus goes with us into the unknown, into challenge, into joy and sorrow alike.

Jesus' presence is not restricted to sacred spaces or formal rituals. He walks with us in kitchens and classrooms, on commutes and in crises. He is there in moments of fear and doubt, in fleeting joys, and in long seasons of transition. He is not only our Savior but our companion—the steady hand beside us when the path seems unclear.

When we understand this, everything changes. Our focus shifts from striving alone to moving in trust, from anxiety over what we cannot control to resting in the One who put the universe into motion. Even when we cannot sense him, even when the world feels loud, chaotic, or uncertain, Jesus remains with us. His companionship is not conditional on our strength, our faith, or our ability to "get it right." It is a gift, intentionally bought and freely given.

Along with comforting us, Jesus' words before ascending also empower us. Because we do not journey alone, our fears, questions, and hopes are carried with him. His presence invites us to live courageously, to act with love, and to extend grace to others, knowing that our Shepherd is eternal, faithful, and victorious. We are not just called to believe in him but to follow him, to embody his love and compassion in the spaces we inhabit each day.

In a world where loneliness, uncertainty, and self-reliance often dominate, this promise grounds us. It reminds us that the God who gave a dying man hope, who protected His mother, and who bore the weight of the cross, walks with us still. His presence is not temporary or symbolic—it is ongoing, active, and life-giving.

Today, Jesus invites us to live with confidence and hope, to move forward with the awareness that we are never alone. He is with us. In every heartbeat, every moment of uncertainty or joy, every small choice and every large turning, his presence is our constant companion. Following him is not a solitary journey—it is a walk hand in hand out of darkness and into light.

"I am *with you* always,
even to the *end* of the age."

Daily Prompts

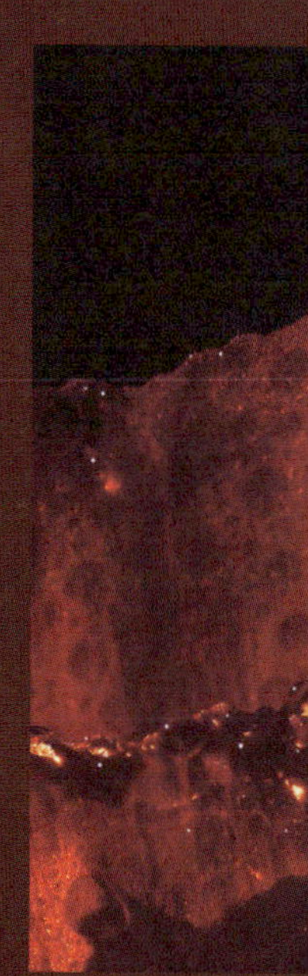

Day 1

Where in life do you most need to feel the presence of Jesus, and how might his promise to be "with you always" bring comfort?

Day 2

How does knowing Jesus is present in ordinary spaces change your perception of daily life?

Day 3

Describe a moment when you sensed Jesus' companionship in a moment of fear, doubt, or uncertainty.

Day 4

How might your awareness of his constant presence influence the way you interact with others?

Day 5

What habits and cues might help you feel Jesus with you, even when you don't sense his presence?

Prayer

Jesus, you walk with me in every moment—seen and unseen, in joy and in struggle. Help me to notice your presence, to trust your guidance, and to live with courage and love. May I carry the assurance of your nearness into all that I do today.

Amen.

TEAM

Brian Chung
Christina Woo
Collin Eldridge
Daniel Han
Ellen Wei
Emaly Tweitmann
Emma Tweitmann
Gabriel Quintanar
John Han
Josh Jang
Josh Yoon
Joyce Tan
Kimberly Huezo
Minzi Bae
Samuel Han
Tyler Zak
Valerie Hui
Willa Jin

LAYOUT DESIGNER	*Janice Park*
PHOTOGRAPHERS	*Ben Pentony* *Corina Straub* *Fiona Rebik* *Heidi Parra* *Jonathan Knepper* *Joyce Chang* *Kayleigh Dyck* *Samuel Han* *Zach Mckinley* *Zorangel Franco*
MODELS	*Corina Straub* *Josh Haddadin* *Lyndsee Farzan*

Continue the conversation
www.alabasterco.com